gr

green

grass

grapes

gray

grandmother
and
grandfather

gr

green